THE DRY VALLEY

THE DRY VALLEY

Bernadette Wagner

POEMS

radiant press

Cover art: Holly Friesen
Book and cover design: Tania Wolk, Third Wolf Studio
Printed and bound in Canada at Friesens, Altona, MB

The publisher gratefully acknowledges the support of
Creative Saskatchewan and the Saskatchewan Arts Board.

creative SASKATCHEWAN

SINCE 1948 SASKATCHEWAN ARTS BOARD

Library and Archives Canada Cataloguing in Publication

Title: The dry valley / Bernadette Wagner.
Names: Wagner, Bernadette L. (Bernadette Lynn), 1962- author.
Identifiers: Canadiana (print) 20190158735 | Canadiana (ebook) 20190158751 | ISBN 9781989274088
(softcover) | ISBN 9781989274095 (PDF)
Subjects: LCGFT: Poetry.
Classification: LCC PS8595.A436 D79 2019 | DDC C811/.6—dc23

radiant press

Box 33128 Cathedral PO
Regina, SK S4T 7X2
info@radiantpress.ca
www.radiantpress.ca

To my loves,
Jim, Kate, and John,
for your love.

PART I : **MIXED GRASSLAND**

PART II : **REGINA, SK**

PART III : **QU'APPELLE VALLEY**

PART I

MIXED GRASSLAND

Playing it Smart

Winter of Grade One.
Boys built a snow hut.
It's for *guy stuff,* not for *girruls.*
But two girls got invited in,
whispered their story in the coatroom after recess.

That night, I remembered
my secret deal with the smart boy. Tippy-toed
to the front porch from the kitchen carrying
the old brown stacking stool, careful
not to clunk when I set it down.
Lifted my pink show'n'tell bag from
my hook and climbed up. My arm

just reaching the red rolled-up
girly calendar Daddy tucked up there
when he came home from the service station
sometime before Christmas.

I slipped the naughty into my sack,
put the stool back, and snuck
to my room. With my treasure under my bed,
I was one step closer to the hand of the boy
who'd walk me into the fort. At least

I wouldn't have to kiss
some dumb boy or stand
in the cold and lift my snow-white undershirt.

After the communal meal

The chatter and walks,
clatter-slam of closing doors,
stockinged feet on polished floors,
kettle's whistled tune,
a teapot's clink and tinging lid of the cookie jar,
scrape of weighted chair,
coughs and sighs, blank-ish stares--

after all this, all
that matters is here-and-now:
the body, that ache,
this breath, my

blue pen in hand, moving across the page,
landing inside the scratch, spill, and stain of thought.

Seeking the poem

In bending bromegrass near the first pine,
east side of the orchard,
a brown mouse scurries
away from footsteps. Breathe.

~

Wind rustles leaves and my nerves.
Alert, I see comfort
in the poetry of sky, its lines stretching end to end,
north to south, east to west. Breathe.

~

Flut-flutter of swallow, cackle of crow,
alarm of chickadees fill the air.
Be with each sense. Breathe.

~

Soft stepping, two white-tailed deer dance, one
passes the last pine, then sashays left
into bush. The second, raising its antlered head,
prances, brushing branches of white raspberries,
crabapple, and Nanking cherry trees, picks
up speed, leaps the fence, and races
into the fallow field. Breathe.

~

Watch worries leave on the rustling
breeze. Walk the path lightly,
into *Silence* at the sixth pine. Breathe.

~

Sitting beneath boughs,
away from hot sun, bring
gratitude for Earth and honouring
the hum of a common fly, let
Mind rest.   Breathe.

It’s one of those times

she thinks she should
probably take care of that mess with the family
papers she’d tucked in the suitcase but every time
she sees what’s there it hurts too much and she’s
tired of all that shit and knows nothing
will change but when

she finally opened the bag and yowled
like a cat locked into a room, let trouble
freefall into consciousness, noted the process
of pen meeting page while that ache
in her chest, that throbbing tight spot beside
her belly, and the always-fiery
hip, shifted – the same time that woman read a poem
about wildflowers along a path and you knew
then and there that she was a poet.

Something in her sharing sparked
a memory. Those flowers, perhaps.
The hint of emotion at the corners
of the eyes. The curve of hip, or maybe
the voice, so strong
but tentative and soft, too, and as gentle
as the easy friendship ever since.
Yes, one of those times.

Enlightenment

From the choir loft I watch
the photographer playing
light on/off on/off around the nave where
an arc strung like Christmas shines and dims
to shine again on some spot beyond her lens,
opposite the purpled altar, and up
toward the ceiling's curves and cornices.

Her flash splits open an intensity so brilliant I slip in,
glimpse a curiousity of curves, supple satin
ruffles behind the folds of here-and-now
disappearing before me.

My will is weak. A sheet of light
envelopes me and I sway,
a million shades of colour rising, falling. Swirling
red, delicate at my feet, dances left, then right,
charges my legs, an electric pulse thickening
through my root and spiraling in a wave of green and pink
to the beat of my heart, into breath and blue voice and up
meeting indigo's wisdom and thought
then bursting out through my crown of glory to shimmer
down and around my gyrating pelvis in a frenzied split second.

I want her to focus
on the Madonna, centred
overhead,
kneeling on red velvet,
a halo of light cast by the dove of peace,
and the angel, Gabriel, on his knees beside her,
a cushion of clouds holding him high.

Desire is an embrace. My lips on hers, our hands
tingle-touch, exploring pleasure in slow, sweet love and longing
tongues tickling this stretch of neck, this wrinkled arm,
that thick leg, the curve of hip, that rib, this rise of breast.

But the photographer shifts back, her third eye seeking
the Holy Mother who carries grief in the robe wrapped
tightly around her. In a halo of light she looks to her dying son.

My right hand cups my aching heart.

Desire is a River, Running

I want to throw my arms around her
know that she longs as much for mine.
I want to say, *sister,* and know it's okay
But I have spent

a lifetime gathering rocks I repeatedly stumble
upon. Never breaking down, never yielding.

How to get
over,
past,
through?

Head to wall, each stone set in place by
my will and still, it does not stop my ache

to lie in the wild with her while
wind blows grasses,
fluffs of white
curves, limbs, trees.

How I long to love you, sister me.

The other side of me

I move within you, light the evening fire
I dip my hands in you and eat your flesh
You are my mirror image and my sister
you disappear like smoke on misty hills
– Diane di Prima

I dip my hands in you and eat her flesh.
I cannot satisfy my hunger.
She disappears like smoke on misty hills.
And when she is gone

I cannot satisfy my hunger;
it growls its need.
When she is gone and
the constant pain of knowing

growls its need
I am Mother bear surviving loss of cub,
-- constant pain of knowing --
always present, perfect in intensity.

I am Mother bear surviving loss of cub,
wanting and missing her
always perfect, present in intensity,
the future tense of what might be.

Wanting and missing her
my world is empty,
the future tense of what might be
love. Come back.

My world, empty.
I move within her, light the evening fire.
Love. Come back,
my mirror image and my sister.

A Caution

Her fingertips brush my arm – accidental
or purposeful? I don't know

what to say, so I lean into
instinct and touch back, matching

her gentleness with my own, saying
yes to evenings wandering backroads

to finding the point where the creek runs
into a ravine and to a bush where birds nest to raise their young.

Beauty in stillness.
When I put my hand into hers

the New Moon raises questions
about tomorrow and tomorrow.

Raindrops or wind can wound
a butterfly's wing.

Too bothered and hot to maintain safe
dialogue, I know animal energy

will take hold and
damage our wings.

Love Song for Emma

Emma Lake, 2002

Oh, Emma, in your presence
I lose language, my composure.
Generations of longing well up,
race my pulse until I swoon and fall--

Oh, Emma,
catch me!

Emma, how you shine--
a sunset of colours bleeding yellow-orange to gold,
blue and green playing to teal while turquoise
commingles with melon,
magenta, cerise.

Oh, Emma,
you blind me!

Emma, how you move--
your esses incite me, your swerves and your curves,
they delight me. Moonrays ripple on water;
night sneaks outside in.

Oh, Emma,
dance me!

So still now, Emma.
So close. Heat on my brow, the nape of my neck,
tingling down my chest, my torso--
I need you. To hell with boundaries!
Let love keep us safe. Trust.

Oh, Emma,
let's go...

Emma, let me pass, take me down
to where your currents run dark and deep.
Let me be the secret you keep.
Yield your darkness.

Share your wild self, that animal beauty,
your curvaceous body,
that love energy.
Then lift me, Emma,
beyond all heights.

Oh, Emma, let me plunge your depths.
ride us to rapture.

Oh, Emma--
Ooh!

Ceres

Pods, once yellow, long, and juicy,
now brown, dry, and shrivelled.

The potential of Ceres alive in each
bold black seed our fingers force out.

We welcome the goddess back to Earth
with heat and humidity, light and time.

She marks her place.
A tender stem reaches up.

Young leaves stretch for Ra.
A strand, tall, with roots holding strong

and tendrils twisting, sticky-wraps support
for blooms and the abundance of harvest.

An ancient ritual. I forget
a single idea's power.

I don't like to think I've lived a Grinch-like life

but I met her and my heart grew
three sizes. That day,

silently sorting seeds from chaff, we planted
friendship and a plan for years of nourishing

conversations and meals, working side-by-side or apart.
Feeding mutual passions for Earth, its beings and ecosystems,

our selves and incorporeal devotion grew. Today, my heart seems too miniscule
to hold all I love about her. How her eyes beam light, crinkle

with crow's toes when joy spreads teeth across her face.
How her vowels elongate and rise in pitch with uncertainties

then settle like evening
while we pluck pea pods from dried stocks, when we load

the recycling onto the back of the truck, and as we haul
a load into town and she eases my anxieties with simple words about weather.

We sit at evening prayers and I know I need a bigger plot for this garden
so I stretch the curves of my heart, promise to honour her and me and the institutions

in which we have chosen to live our lives -- she, married to the church,
me, a monogamous marriage -- as we tend our friendship vine, watch it wind

around and through the conventions that threaten to confine and keep us
ordered by grids and toxins, and pray we can find our way

to the bloom of heart where each of us
remains committed to our vows.

The unfinished poem

is the suite I will write
when I get a minute

doesn't trust me, tags
behind, in disguise

nags, pretends
to be whole

takes a stool at the bar,
orders a crantini, extra olives

trips me up on grammar, dangling
participles, mixed modifiers

leaves for the coast, late one night, holding
my cash for the bag of inspiration she left to pick up

eventually admits defeat.

Griefwork

When you told me you'd cried
the night your brother died
that moment became an intimate detail
more cherished than the porcelain cup
that travelled three continents and five generations
to find me.

I imagine his leaving took a chunk
of you big enough to replaster the walls and fill the cracks
and gaps in this slum landlord's building.

When you encase your tender heart
in cement and I do not have a sledgehammer
I throw words.

Learning to Sew

Before grade one starts, Auntie
takes hold of the fabric, shakes
out wrinkles while the tape measure jiggles,
uneven, around her neck. She snaps
the fold into place and lays the paisley cloth
on her dining room table then pins
thin pieces of paper, marked with words
and lines I cannot read. But I know
my letters and numbers, see A and B and C
and 1 and 2. And then she scissors
the paper, stopping to go around
the dark diamond bumps that tell her where to put
the pieces together. I'm too small
to cut, she says. Her scissors are very sharp.
So I watch until the last one is cut.
Her needle and thread mark special spots
she needs to line up buttons and darts that don't have points.
Soon she is at the sewing machine, not the old
foot pump one, but her new one, the electric.
And she's zipping along. No swear words
from her, not like when Mommy's sewing.

She tells me to try it on. But there's no sleeves,
I say, The picture has sleeves. And she laughs,
tells me they'll come later. She needs to
make sure this fits, first. I think it does.
But she pinches the joined parts
and says it needs to come in
a bit at the yoke. Whatever that is.
There's no eggs here so
I do as I'm told, take it off and get dressed.
Auntie sews some more and I colour in
her book of animals. Enough she says
after a while. It's time to make supper.
When I look at her, she says not to worry,
we'll do more later. We'll have it done
before Mom comes to pick me up tomorrow.
And it is.

PART II

REGINA SK

You live here

I could pretend you are not here, you who grabs a six-pack
each night after work, always sure to hold back

pleasure until the old beater is perfectly parked
in the driveway, behind the 74 Westy

until the house key turns the lock
and hangs on the hook to rest,

until the tunes are cranked,
the slippers on, and your Archie Bunker chair

perfectly adjusted, before
you twist the top.

I can't leave you

alone with the kids, can't trust
your sense to be common enough

to stop after one or two,
that you'd change diapers or put

our babies to bed with pyjamas on,
that your cigarette would not burn

our old couch, the new carpet,
my books, my loves.

I could leave

let you drink yourself drunk
like my now-dead uncles did,

watch you grow
into their slobbering echo.

I can't decide

but if the Louise Hay types are right
and these sizzling hips are a manifestation

of my inability to move forward
perhaps the Demerol the doctor's

dripping into my veins will
stimulate an idea to free me

from clothing carpeting the floors,
dishes piled high both sides of sink,

fridge stuffed full
of rotting leftovers,

this bleak life.

Wisdom*

This old elm, having offered her leaves
to Earth in a frenzy, stands naked.
Ancient ritual of letting go.

Spruce never bare limbs unless dead or dying.
New blue needles grace the tips of soft,
sagging boughs. Each year's collection of cones
falls into winter.

                    Snowflakes pile high
in the flower box. Spent blooms of seeds
we planted stand atop stems strong and crystalline,
nurtured in the soil we wheeled from the compost bin
you built in the backyard for me.

That was when
our work filled the air and the blend of Nicotinia and sweat eventually
released passion in those short nights. Still flowering
at summer's end, Lobelia dropped
down past purple pansies, trailing. Tonight, supporting
that drift of white behind the rippled window panes. And the frames
surrounding, cedar-stained, matted with rime, play
the street's light, bending in the glittery night to reveal
a secret, silver staircase over the weathered plants,
above trees, beyond misted rooftops, to the sparkled sky –

an invitation to climb,
to find the cold clear jewel that's waiting
somewhere past the near-full moon, further, beyond a strange planet
in another galaxy, shining. To find the star

that will
expire
with me.

*after *Cantilevered songs* by John Lent

You give me so much space between words

You drown grief
pour amber from brown bottles.

I am noosed with debt,
fierce

politics, and bad poetry.
Uncertainty clouds me.

When we found each other
my fear pushed you away.

~

Isn't intimacy more than
    our arms draped
    over each other, legs
        entwined each night before sleep,

the kisses you drop
    on my lips every morning before you walk
        out the door to catch the 7:45,

emailed grocery lists, items
    I'd forgotten: milk, baking soda, fresh carrots,
        or a full meal, deal or otherwise,

or the tender meat and mashed potatoes I prepare
    despite my vegetarianism and the beans
        and lentils you tolerate because of it,

more than lists,
  our household tasks; you, laundry, me,
    family and social calendars; you, dishes and counters;
      me, food in detail: planning, purchase, planting,
        growth, preservation; you, motors
          and engines, wood and construction; or not, and
            we let our fingers walk through yellow pages,

  our bodies
    feeding primal needs,
      becoming one, coming,

more than, and all, this?

~

Something restrains me. What,
I cannot name.

~

Sometimes, you are the poem I want
to write. Long, lingering lines about
to break, like my heart, when
your silence goes on for pages and I

cannot read your complex equations, your form.
Your pattern is a manuscript shapeshifting. I may never find
resolution. A solution escapes me

so I freewrite my self into what I think you need, forget
my own needs until I am ready

to explode, then wonder if there is room enough
in this marriage for me. How much do I need

the vast space between your words?

Rant

(in memory of the Stephen Harper regime)

I wanted to stop the bus, get off, and walk
wherever she's walking, talk
whatever she's talking because I was so hot-
damn interested in what she'd said about

the possibility of us making a difference in this
world, on a planet where the largest
enterprise in our history as a species spills
and kills trees and fish and people,

births two-headed moose calves, toxicifies
birds and communities and families left
to swim in the aftermath of the path ploughed
by the drill baby drill creed called

progress, a progress that profits the already
wealthy in a country corporatized,
its people monopolized by the language
of luxury and tyrannized by an illegitimate

government, robocalled into office by
an electorate living in the fear of reprisal,
a state ruled by capital and a system
gone rotten, like Denmark when

Shakespeare penned plays for the people.
I worried this melancholic nation would never
collect midnight weeds from the field
and invoke Hecate's storm.

We met for coffee

She walked toward me and
just before I kissed her lips she turned
her cheek, expecting the more European familiarity
but I quickly met her lips full-on and breathed more easily.
I didn't explain how much I had needed that, not sexual
desire but arising from a deeper place.

So when I thought
I read embarrassment
and shock in the rise of
her perfect bright green eyes,
the shimmering light around her,
the girlish giggle and a clarification
voiced loudly, "Oh, what a lovely way
to meet in the morn! A kiss on the lips,
full-on, and a big hug, too." I wondered
if she was taken aback or thrilled – or
perhaps just a bit of both. Because

there's something visceral in her
core energy that speaks to me,
but not in the way in which
most humans are accustomed.
It's in the body's power
to exist in time and space.

Missed shot

I walk in on his attempt to sink a stripe
in the far left corner. He lifts his eyes, pushes the cue
which slips off *The Lady* and the cue ball
kisses a solid, nearly scratches.
His grin, as lopsided as his shot, signals
he's seen me chuckling. Straightens his long
lean body. Sidles toward me.
Smirk dances on his champagned face.

I've known this stranger for centuries. Danced

this one before – different time, different place.
He calls me *sweetheart,* encircles
my waist with his business casual arm, pulls me close.
When he puckers his lips I survey
the room filled with people I know,
turn my head just enough to allow
his lips to connect with my cheek
then fret I've hurt his feelings.

But I know he'll be the one moving on.
So when he asks, *Where's the boyfriend?*
I reply, *Home, with the kids.*
Hold my tears in.

Takeover

You love that ‘74 Westy. I overhear you.

Well, after I got the fuel pump and oil filter mount out
I had to pull out the lifters and keep them straight.

I lean into the doorjamb. Your hands reach down and lift up.

Then, I had one bitch of a time
getting all the 13mm nuts and bolts off.
And the half dozen 15mm main bearing bolts, too.
But those were easier.
You have to hold the case halves
together while you do it. So I got them all out,
or so I thought, tapped all around the case halves
with that small hammer -- the one with the black handle --
and pulled. Hard as I could. Like a son-of-a-bitch.

Your hands rise.
Crows’ feet thicken around your eyes.
Your cheeks bulge.
Your lips form a thin line.

I tapped and pulled for I don’t know how goddamned long.
Goddamn thing, it would not give.
So I looked again
and there’s the goddamn 13mm nut I missed.

Your right index finger
makes a little circle on the tabletop.

Hiding deep in a hole on the right side and covered in grease.
Took the damned thing out and bingo, she comes apart--
kinda like Mom did when she found it in the dishwasher later.

You look at me with a smirk.

Taco Dinner

You must be proud of him, she says, *For taking this on.*
Our old friend pours tea from flowered porcelain.
My cheeks flush hot. *Learning to take it apart,*
fixing it, and putting it back together again.

Long weeks of you engaged,
again, not with me. The van this time.
Better than booze and bottles.
Greasy auto parts, toxic smells linger
in our studio garage. Was it really
my idea to jointly use the space?

He's such a smart man. Dedicated.
She looks to me as though I should respond.

Were my shouts about the oily part
you called a "taco plate" and ran
through the dishwasher called for?
When I announced
that dishes would be done by hand until the dishwasher
was scrubbed clean and the smell gone, and that I
wouldn't do it,
was that really "over-the-top"?

Rebuilding it on his own
instead of paying somebody to do it.
I raise the hot cup to my lips.

Fantasyland

Far from jizz-coated keyboards and screens
in thousands of dark rooms and offices
around the globe, she plays her game,

inspiring remains that would light up
a circle of semen should an infrared light shine
on the members of her audience.

Erotic movie? Four cowboy outlaws offer a choice:
Watch us rape your daughters or let us
all have you. Four times, raped.

Her 250 viewers rub their way
to orgasm while she rides
a dildo to freedom.

Spring Thaw

I thought of her at Sexsmith Road and again
when the *No Vacancy* sign flashed
icing pink at the Moonlight Motel and strains
of hurtin' tunes wafted on the air. Why
the onslaught of lonesome and well of tears?
No circular rhythm of a whippoorwill this far north.
No whining midnight train across the lake.
No moon hiding a face behind a cloud.

Less than twenty-four hours since we said goodbye –
it's not as though we're particularly close
but, across the table, when
she introduced me to her passion, the planets and stars
moved and realigned, Mercury's retrograde ended,
and Saturn returned. Her eyes turned
the room emerald, awakened something
in me as sharp and sweet as ice melting in spring.

The body remembers

It's a blade teasing my arm, a white lie,
the line of possibility quickening.
My body remembers, memoryfog –
a quivering spine, the fragment

go away, i can't even –

but there he is and here i am and i can't
and there's blood so much. Bloody
hurting pieces of me shivering.

red cheeks hot, hold tears.
can't cry, crybaby.

Yes, you can, little one,
that line from his finger to you, nothing
compared to the three pointing back at him.

Rage! Rage!
March! March!
Injustice!
Privileged male power

A courtroom. The accused, quiet,
while accusers endure dissection.
No perfect witness in a survivor.

The headline should read:
Urgent actions taken in response
to study by Stats Canada
4 in 5 women live
with personal knowledge
of a sexual crime.

Our voices loud.
Our body remembering.

Inside-out

They're looking into my window, I know, but
I don't seem able to give much of a damn, not
that way, anyway. I mean, yes, surveillance
state and all, but when my curtains are open

and I'm prancing around naked because I am
in my house and I forgot to
take the new bar of soap up the stairs
or my favourite towel, the one

that's in the dryer, down two flights.
I'm prancing around, naked,
in my house and if I am
seen because someone glances in from the street

or the backyard or the houses across, front,
back, or either side, well, hello, here I am!
Living with my eyes opened wide to what's
coming in and I am not going

to apologize for the revelation into who I am, what I
believe. And the freedom to do
as I please, so long as I harm no other.

Judgement has no place here, inside the window I freely
give. Yes, it is deep and dark in here, yes, I
know. No room for shame, here.
There is room for only the deep and abiding

love we share inside and out.

Waking up

Clarity comes long after the stage
light landed on my head, jarring
my neck and life out of alignment. Concussion,
the doctors said. A month to heal. Not
really. Not days or weeks. Not even
months. So much is broken.

> *Full stop. Anger in*
> *everything. How to be*
> *helpless in a go-go-go world?*

Doctors feed me dreams
laced with valium. Fitful nights of morphine.
The mind wants what it wants.

> *A newspaper comic*
> *lightbulb in a thought bubble:*
> HELP, *small font, all caps, question mark.*

Tingles run shoulder to head, ending
in sharp shots, landing again and
again, pulsing pain numbed by a medley
of meds. I text message for water and food
and wonder if sex will ever be possible again.

> *Movement of neurons, impossible. Thought*
> *hurts. No one understands. It's not me*
> *not caring; it's me not thinking.*

I want to chop carrots, onions, celery, unheeded.
Un-needed, arm won't work.
Simple sums, logic, small household
tasks, the pen across a page – a no-go.

Hello? Don't you care?
Can I love enough to let others in?

Everything's wrong, the cooking, the cleaning,
all of it. They don't understand. I don't
want to shout, don't want to cry.

"Love is patient and kind," he said.

My head throbs with love
for their acts of love.

Weeding the Garden

I start at the outside edges
where the light is bright, work in
on a spiral toward darker parts.

Perennial grasses push
the edges of my patience, rampant

root re-generation overtaking beds of
meditative practice where once insight

blossomed purple, fuschia, yellow.
I dig deep. A garden fork

perpendicular to the ground,
tines prying as I angle up

releasing long-held tears.
Toss the clump

into rusted wheelbarrow,
push it to the compost heap.

At the edge

I could have pushed her
away yet again when she said,
You can, if you want.

But I couldn't have stopped myself
from fitting my curves into hers,
letting our lips linger

ever so gently until she
pulled the longing from me

with the scent of her so-soft skin
and we leaned in, tongues

intertwining in a rushing
tingle that overtook common sense.
Lipstick long-gone, my breath

short, I couldn't have stopped
that full-bodied plea.

In the hour after

I confess to what you will perceive as an adulterous act there is

cacaphony, a murder of crows,

your finger, pointing,

a buzzing overhead,

green shoots from brittle brown,

a White Admiral's barred wings, dancing,

a string of giggling children, sandwiched by two adults,

black-dotted orange wings, spreading,

the rustling leaves,

silence.

PART III

QU'APPELLE VALLEY

Morning on the Lake

When I wake her, my daughter's face is sunlight
piercing my dark thoughts. We groggy-step the gravelled road,
veer off at the saskatoon patch and cut through bushes
down the path by Monument Hill, careful
on the slippery descent into Temple Park.

We catch glimpses of the lake from the long-abandoned railway bed
that once transported people and supplies to this
summer village and beyond. Before six a.m. we slip the silver
into the lake, push past the children's slide.

The pink-gray sky ripples when
our paddles cut calm waters, propel
us past buoys, boathouses, marsh.

Gliding south, beyond grebes wandering the sand,
far past Landslide Hill and toward the beaver dam,
our canoe stays parallel to the shore, or tries to.
Water and sky grow silver-gray.
Arms and shoulders know what to do:
quiet jay-stroke. Imperfect,
but a cross-bow corrects.

Paddles across the gunwales, we rest, scan the hills.
Behind us, dark clouds creep closer. Portside, sunrise dims.
My daughter points to the yellow-brown ridge on the right, where
the dip and rise of a three-pointed stag silhouettes
blue-gray. *Berries? Luscious grass?*

At the dam we turn around. Waves slap
the nose of our craft. Wind wields
her pony-tail like a whip. An ache fingers my back.
Our wake is esses connected as we counter the current that pulls
us south, away from the blue slide near the distant shore.

The stitch in my shoulder screams. Terns screech
as we round an orange buoy. We shiver
toward shore, scrape sand, tug
the canoe to land, collapse
on the sand, curve into each other, wrapped
in an old blanket from Luella's Gift
as we watch a beaver glide by.

Above, the sky is smoke-gray.
Does my body remember?
Oh, yes.

Luella's Gift

The kids learn the thrill.
Outside shower on the side of a treed hill,
two scooped hands filled with slick black muck from the bottom of the lake,
sand-castle buildings and dreams. Undertows and drop-offs, quick
sand-walking on plus-thirty days, skipping stones, several
times with a simple wrist-flick. The blue-green
of algae, scratch of *the itch,* waspy stings. Poison
oak, nettle, and sunburn. Aroma
of skunk, outhouse, that rotting carcass in the bush.

And grief, they learn, too. For
the lot down the hill that's been shaved
for new construction. The multiple
costs of the multimillion dollar development going on
across the lake. How penny candies become a thing of the past.

They learn joy in befriending the only other child on the beach, and in
no time, know the child's name, and the path to their cottage
based on proximity to the park and the store, and will show you.
The joys of sandpail and shovel, sticks
and stones, castles and moats, of hide'n'seek tag,
and Manitoba Maple leaf flags, they learn, too.

They learn the land, mudslides and chimneys, when
and where to pick berries -- saskatoon and
chokecherry ripened near-black -- and the magical

transformation into muffins and pies, syrups and jams,
the names for goldfinch, chickadee, and flicker
by sight, and the song of the mourning dove almost all the day long,
to identify stars, constellations, and planets, and know the moon's phases
beyond teachers teachings, to weather and the clouds overhead
and to pay attention to thunderheads that bring light-shows and rain.
They learn the language of deer and of tree, rocks and dreams, to
go to sleep early, sleep late, sleep any time at all, nestled
in a corner, swinging in the hammock, curled
up in a bed or stretched out on the beach,
a book close at hand.

Fieldnotes from the Qu'Appelle

(in memory of Robert Kroetsch)

Morning bursts apricot and yellow
on the lake. Gray driftwood floats on sky.
White sails, a blue breeze.

~

Water gurgles, chugs.
Beeps announce coffee.

This place allows
for human
and more-than-human connection.

Wings, skin,
bark, fur co-exist.

~

Just around the bend,
maybe three miles north
somewhere between the hills
hanging

in a mist that curves
around land and heart,
insistent wind holds hawk high.
She swoops

drops

then climbs, feast tightly taloned.
Soars over trees, birds, insect,
over chattering squirrels,
water, blood.

~

Number Eleven highway,
two blades slicing skin,
how progress scalped this valley.

~

Two turkey vultures spiral high,
closer, closer to the hillside
abattoir.

~

Orange-breasted robin pecks apart huge moth.
Families of swallows, inhaling insects, dip,
rise, dip again.

~

Qu'Appelle Valley green is
silver sage,
a treetop's lime,
river bank hay,
market garden crops,
stands of spruce, stretching,
short commercial lawn,
sea of forest holding a hill,
a yellow clover stalk.

~

Living sky
shapeshifts colours,
a river of vulnerability
pinpricked by light.

~

Peace filters through
singing elms,
beneath their fluttering gold,
rippling grasses.

Learning Bird

We put on the hoods of our stories
and fly inward – Phil Hall

Bees bury their bodies in blooms.
Each purple monkshood stem is a chorus singing praises.

Chickadees peck at the bark of the elms that shade
the short path to the outhouse until one dee-dees a warning.

A grouse gives a ruffle--
sharptailed or ruffed, I don't know.

I leave the door wide-open, the scent of our shit floating on the breeze.
I make a mental note to buy limestone dust next trip into town.

But honestly, the door is open to bear witness to the world.
Why close it out?

Today, my tears freely fall. Leslie's death is that constant ache
in my chest for the time she spent loving everyone,

especially children, as an auntie does, and
painting a poem on the outhouse walls.

I take *A Field Guide to the Birds*, the 25th Impression, April 1958,
from the shelf, rippling pages to determine differences

between grouse and wild chickens. I know so little
about my place, I lift my hood in praise.

Mallard Love

Between the thru and turning lanes, a duck
as still as the one I didn't find one summer
after I'd raced around the curve
just before the valley, just seven klicks from here

not that I'd stopped.
It wasn't in my rearview mirror
when I slowed down to glance.

Catching the corner of a speeding car, a bird would likely
die on contact, flip
over the guardrail, flop down the steep side into the bushes
like a chicken beheaded.

I didn't really care. Not until today
when rounding the corner
a mallard flew over, solo.
Mallards are typically monogamous.

Holding on

This is my heart, gently
curved by a childhood on rolling hills,
despite barbed wire.

That is the valley, the ups
and downs that further shaped me.
Today's diminished light, longer
shadows, shines red and golden bright.

Grasses now taupe, turning
to silver. The sky,
a backdrop of blue they call azure -- I call sky-blue --
with white blowing by.

Gusts grow greater and greater still.
The wires sing alcoholic blues.
A ladybug holds tight to the *bastard toadflax* as
I hold onto you.

Mapping the Poem

Hot peri-menopausal afternoon,
sweaty sun pulsing love

in me. Alongside, the silvergray pasture
floats. Inside the a/c cools

my sunlit arm, my chest, ruffles
my hair. I am cool when we gather

in the gallery. Our expressions, witnessed,
as we interconnect with All Beings*,

the confluence of creatures
strung and hung among all that is now.

~

We writers scratch ideas.
Words meet paper. Art

feeds art. Upcycled sheers, wheat-pasted
with colour and content, long

and narrow manifestations of Beings
called into Presence through meditation

and reverence, a guided practice of seeing,
being, and creating. Representations

of Artemis, Diana, Fauna, Gaia, Flora, Salacia,
inhabitants of this place, this time beyond time –

this moment –
fills two rooms.

~

My creation is not yet hung;
it's growing in me like a poem, not yet

much more than a string of words
those lost on the tip of a tongue, not

ready for expression, not yet
a concept complete enough to explore.

~

But I explored, brushwork
urgently reminding me that the skills required

for crafting poems do not necessarily transfer
to painting on sheer fabric lying flat along two tables. Still,

a narrative, winding and long like the creek,
Wolverine, takes shape and leads me

to the lake. Last Mountain Lake, long
and lean, where innumerable generations of children

splashed and feared, loved and revered.
It's what I should have painted. Yes,

should – the perfectionist's mantra.
I can give rein to words. No, not words, exactly,

perhaps more the languages, the language of the
human and more-than-human beings that

dwell in our spheres, known and unknown, visible
to the naked eye or microscopic wavelengths of

energy moving in and around us. The Beings, hanging
in Confluence among us, all welcome, all here

to witness not fear but the fearlessness as necessary
as breath to give oneself over to the otherness that

can be found in the throes of creation – and not just
the otherness of the every day artist's practice

kind of angst but the deep-down deliciously dirty
work of revealing the bones, the what's holding me

up on this walk around the block
with your sweater over my arm.

* *All Beings Confluence* is an art installation managed by textile artist Martha Cole.

The Dry Valley

Running good, you say, your
eyes that bright blue that made me love you,
your satisfaction with the 74 Westy widening the distance
between your moustache and beard.
I meet you with my own grin.
Yup, say I. *Well done!*

Rows of houses, transplanted trees and
smoking stacks shrink in the hot haze.
Fields of canola yellow,
green-gold acres of wheat wave us on,
black fallow and farm yards fly by
on my right. On my left
your hands steer a gentle curve as
we hum along, Dire Straits' *Brothers in Arms*
crackling from the van's old cassette stereo

It saved you, this van.
Your taking off that part like a bottle cap
and putting it back on tight,
dismantling and rebuilding
this engine, yourself, saved us.

That day I sank into the wingback chair, deciding,
the kids finally asleep in their beds, you
passed out and snoring on our old wine couch.
The dishwasher rumbling its discontent from the kitchen.
The fan's oscillation blowing repeated whiffs of stale beer
from the half-full bottle I'd rescued from your hand and the empties
scattered on our second-hand coffee table.

And then, the stack of clothing on the stool beside me
announced its lemony freshness. If I'd
packed up our children and left that night
I doubt you'd have figured it out until late the next day.

We round another curve, descend into the Qu'Appelle,
where drought lives in the pale greens and faint browns
of the hillsides. A hard year. You shift
down from 4th to 3rd as we climb the other side.
The old Westy holds at 90 klicks, running smoothly,
the dry valley now behind us.

Weathering the storm

Early February on the Canadian plains;
tawny, auburn, and gold stalks shimmer
on the valley floor. Their white blankets should
have arrived months ago but even an hour
north, where trees and hills curve a light blue horizon,
the cover is moth-eaten over sun-yellow stubble.

Rains will have to bring life. Unless Earth
requires more time to recover from last year's
floods, those that leaked through our foundation.

Instead of being upfront with you, instead
of saying, *I don't know if I can do this,*
I danced that edge of wanting/not
wanting, knowing/not knowing, new/
not new sensations quivering my body,
pushing boundaries that both thrilled
and set the fight/flight reaction in motion

until I felt forced to choose. And I did
want to see if happiness with you,
now sober, was possible.

New Moon

The front step creaks. Screen door squeaks.
One breath tingle-traces a shivering
line of temptation up and down my spine.

My silly giggle almost ruins the moment but
when you scanned the full length of my body,
nude, under a long, sheer, black shirt,

your pants immediately tighten
at the crotch and I can't help
but appreciate my cunning.

You stand, stunned. I lay back,
ruby-lipped and spread-eagled, on the leather sofa,
a pornographic cliché you hadn't anticipated.

Your tongue wets your lips.
The zipper has to open soon.
As you come to me my right hand

whisper-touches skin, spiralling
fingertips around hardened nipples,
dancing down torso to part labia.

You almost drop your guitar
in the rush to quench your thirst.
Such a long, dry summer,

you fall to your knees
and drink my love.

Eternal love *

I drift among the calling lights of night, ignoring
your snoring and the breeze that goose-bumps my back.
I do not lift my hand to pull up the covers.

The exquisite bend of your thumb and forefinger
on my sensitive nipple, the arc of your palm and wrist
holding the curve and weight of my breast,

my cupped hand on your now-soft scrotum,
yesterday's long ache of desire, fulfilled,
fuels two beings love-locked in a dream

from which neither will awake,
their love is committed and practiced
until their last breaths expire,

their souls rush out,
and the journey to each other
begins anew.

*after *Jitterbug Perfume* by Tom Robbins

Acknowledgements

This manuscript would not have been possible without the Saskatchewan Writers' Guild's and the programs, services, and opportunities it provides, including the St. Peter's Retreats, Manuscript Evaluation Service, and its publications. Sage Hill Writing also provided much-needed and much-appreciated time and guidance in the creation of this manuscript. The Last Mountain Lake Cultural Centre in Regina Beach, Saskatchewan, allowed me valuable time to write during my term as the inaugural literary artist-in-residence at their facility. As well, the Saskatchewan Arts Board's assistance was a welcome support.

My gratitude extends to Lorna Crozier for a long-ago conversation in a hallway at St. Peter's Abbey, to Brenda Schmidt, Elizabeth Bachinsky, Dave Margoshes, and Sean Virgo for their feedback on earlier versions of the work and to Ken Babstock and Betsy Warland for much wisdom and support in its fine-tuning. To my dream of an editor, Kimmy Beach, thank you for your careful eye, wise words, and pep talks. To Larry Hall, Jeff Nye, Kristen Teetaert, and the communities near the southern shore of Last Mountain Lake – thank you for the opportunity to serve you. Thanks also to B Print Ink, the Last Mountain Lake Cultural Centre, Of Land and Sky (Sask Outdoor Education Society), and The Society (St. Peter's College) for publishing some of these poems.

Last, but certainly not least, to my family and friends near and far: without you and your ongoing kindnesses, love, and patience, as well as encouragement over the long haul, I would never be a writer, let alone have completed this body of work. I am truly blessed.

Bernadette Wagner, writer, editor, and community based educator, has recent work in Absent Mothers (DP: 2017) and *Without Apology: Writings on Abortion* in Canada (AUP: 2016). Her poetry and nonfiction have been broadcast on radio and TV, recorded on video and film, and published in magazines and anthologies. Shortlisted for the Saskatchewan First Book Award, she toured *This hot place* (Thistledown, 2010), her first poetry collection, across the country. An activist for social justice, a spokesperson for various feminist organizations, a founder of the Prairie Lily Feminist Society and Friends of Regina Public Library, a board member for the Saskatchewan Writers Guild and Sage Hill Writing Experience, a past Literary Co-ordinator and two-time Chair of the Cathedral Village Arts Festival, and the inaugural literary artist-in-residence at the Last Mountain Lake Cultural Centre. Bernadette lives in Regina, Saskatchewan.